EXECUTIVE
FOUNDATION
5 Essential Skills for Senior Leaders

BY

VAL WILLIAMS
AND ELLEN FREDERICKS

EXECUTIVE FOUNDATION: 5 ESSENTIAL SKILLS FOR
SENIOR LEADERS
Published by Shadowbrook Publishing
P.O. Box 2458
Edison New Jersey 08818

Library of Congress Control Number:2005901238

ISBN: 0-9712007-6-9

ACKNOWLEDGEMENTS

We'd like to thank the following people without whom this book would not look as good as it does: Susan Meigs our editor; Mike Cox our book cover designer; and Marie Schulz our assistant extraordinaire.

EXECUTIVE FOUNDATION PROGRAM

The Five Skills of a Successful Leader

What do successful executives have in common? They have built a strong Executive Foundation: they have acquired the skills, behaviors, and perspectives that drive great performance and results. The Executive Foundation™ Program is designed for seasoned, new or aspiring executives to assess and improve the strength of their own executive foundation: the essential skills that reflect many of the attributes of successful senior leaders. We have identified the following five key skills as the foundation of a senior executive's success:

- Visioning
- Aligning
- Strategizing/Planning
- Executing
- Developing People

This program will help you gauge your degree of strength for each skill, identify any gaps or weaknesses, and work on gaining mastery. From our experience working with hundreds of executives, we have found that executives who master these five skills generally are more successful. The benefits of using the Executive Foundation Program include:

BETTER RESULTS

In today's fast paced business world, who doesn't need to achieve better results? This may look like greater revenue, more profit, higher customer satisfaction, faster time to market, reduced costs, or higher employee retention and satisfaction. A stronger executive foundation increases the probability that you can go beyond expected results.

LESS STRESS

Many of our clients say that they are working harder than ever before with fewer resources and higher expectations of what they need to deliver. Building your executive foundation will help to increase your strategizing and planning skills so that you can be more proactive and get ahead of the curve. When you are ahead of the curve you have more control, which means less stress.

INCREASED STABILITY

Many of our clients say that they are frustrated trying to keep up with ever changing goals and business conditions. Yet this lack of stability is often caused by internal factors such as poor long-term planning rather than by changes in external industry conditions. Executives who master the skills of visioning, strategizing and planning will create greater stability in their work environments.

DECREASED CONFLICT

Executives whose strategies, plans and goals for their organization are linked to a clear vision will have an organization that is working towards a common purpose. Having a clear, well thought-out vision linked to immediate strategies and plans reduces the likelihood of conflict, since key stakeholders will be aligned on what is required and expected of them.

IMPROVED PERFORMANCE

Executives with a strong executive foundation oversee organizations that run like well oiled machines. Everything and everyone is in sync and there are few if any breakdowns in plans and procedures. Imagine leading an organization in which you are proactive versus reactive; know where you are heading for the next 1-3 years; have everyone aligned on plans and goals; have adequate resources; execute with quality and therefore deliver the results you want.

How satisfied are you with your own Executive Foundation? Take the Executive Foundation Assessment to find out.

THE EXECUTIVE FOUNDATION ASSESSMENT
Instructions for Completing the Assessment:

1. Answer each question.
2. If the statement is true all of the time or most of the time, check the box.
 (Do not answer "true" or check the box if the statement is only "sometimes" true.)
3. Total your checkmarks for each skill area.
4. Set your standards high when answering the questions. Be tough on yourself.

SKILL 1: VISIONING

☐ I have a vision that reflects my values. It is an ideal future that is exciting to work towards.

☐ I can articulate the vision in a way that others can understand and remember.

☐ I have written down the vision and it is posted in public areas of the organization.

☐ I have gotten feedback about the vision from all levels of the organization.

☐ The most junior person in my organization can describe our vision.

☐ My direct reports have articulated what the organizational vision has in common with their personal vision and values.

☐ My vision is reflected in our strategic planning sessions and is what we use to make decisions about priorities.

☐ I create excitement in others by talking about the vision. It is a call to action.

☐ My organization uses a regular measurement tool to see how well we live the vision.

☐ The vision supports the company's purpose and sustains the company's profitability.

_____ **Total**

SKILL 2: ALIGNING

☐ My vision is reflected in our hiring practices, our business planning, our performance management, and our compensation systems.

☐ I regularly meet with business partners and colleagues to build relationships and discuss their concerns and needs.

☐ I regularly meet with key business partners and colleagues to discuss our vision and objectives.

☐ I know when someone on my team is not aligned with our vision and objectives.

☐ I take immediate action when a team member's actions are out of alignment with our vision.

☐ I understand how everyone contributes to the vision and objectives of our organization.

☐ I meet with my team regularly to evaluate where our strategies and activities align with our vision and where they do not.

☐ My team functions like a well-oiled machine.

☐ People on my team feel comfortable discussing when things are going off track.

☐ I sell my vision to senior management, my peers, and my team.

_____ **Total**

SKILL 3: STRATEGIZING/PLANNING

☐ I know the top 3-5 goals that my team must accomplish this year to be successful.

☐ I know the short-term strategies that will get us there.

☐ I have a business plan to achieve these goals.

☐ I have well-developed contingency plans for my primary goals.

☐ My knowledge of industry conditions affecting my business is current.

☐ We regularly discuss and update our business plan and objectives.

☐ I am aware of the obstacles that may interfere with accomplishing our collective goals.

☐ I invite and am open to new ideas on how to achieve our goals.

☐ I encourage open conversation and debate about issues that affect our team's dynamics and objectives.

☐ We know how we will measure our success.

____ **Total**

SKILL 4: EXECUTING

☐ My daily actions and decisions match/model my personal values and standards.

☐ We have established operating standards and norms that support our team.

☐ We follow the policies and processes that we have established.

☐ My staff has adequate resources to accomplish their goals.

☐ I take time to acknowledge and affirm people informally and have established a formal reward and recognition system.

☐ We use clear measurement and tracking systems to monitor individual and team success.

☐ We manage to an annual operating budget.

☐ We use an incentive system that is linked to our strategies and goals.

☐ We have clear roles and responsibilities and clear accountability for each deliverable.

☐ We consistently meet or exceed our goals and objectives.

_____ **Total**

SKILL 5: DEVELOPING PEOPLE

☐ I build rapport with my team members beyond business issues.

☐ I am fair and treat people equally. I don't have favorites.

☐ I communicate key information quickly to my team.

☐ People say that I am approachable and accessible. Members of my team trust me.

☐ I invest in relationships with people at all levels within my organization.

☐ People say that I am a good listener.

☐ I empower members of my team. I tell them what needs to be accomplished, not how it needs to be done.

☐ I am adept at making people right when giving critical or difficult feedback .

☐ I regularly ask for feedback from my staff, my peers, and my manager.

☐ I challenge and coach people to a higher level of performance.

_____ **Total**

Charting Your Progress

Step 1: Identify strengths

What are you already good at? In which areas did you score the highest? It is important to identify your strengths and build on them. The Gallup Organization defines a strength as near perfect performance in an activity, which you must be able to repeat consistently. In our coaching terminology, we describe a strength as an activity that you are masterful at. So using this criteria, select your top three skills that you consider strengths.

Step 2: Identify areas for development

Areas for development could be strengths that you already have but underutilize. Or you might have skills that you feel are average that you want to sharpen. Or, of course, there might be weak areas that you need to improve. Which skills do you most want to develop? Do you need to make a shift in perspective? What do you want to master? To help you focus, choose three items to start with, then, once you have mastered them, tackle three more.

STEP 3: WORK WITH YOUR COACH

Use your coach to help you to develop the areas you have identified and to take advantage of your current strengths. Your coach can help you make shifts in perspective, practice new skills, and overcome obstacles until you can give yourself that checkmark!

STEP 4: TRACK YOUR PROGRESS

Use the Progress Chart that follows to record your scores in each area over a period of time. Complete the questions once a quarter, for example, to measure your improvement.

STEP 5: PRACTICE

Practice the behaviors that will strengthen your performance until they have become part of your leadership style. The goal is to eventually be able to check off every box on the assessment. Let's say, for example, you want to be better at visioning. The first step is to make visioning a priority as you move forward and set up new goals, initiatives and projects. Seek out a trusted colleague who can help you craft a vision for your organization. Or work with your direct reports to come up with a vision that reflects what you collectively most value and see for the future. If you want to be better at strategizing you'll need to take time out with your team to develop a strategic plan. In that session you can practice listening to and generating new ideas, identifying obstacles to your goals and planning contingencies.

Keep this assessment in a visible location where you can refer to it regularly and use the questions as a checklist.

PROGRESS CHART

(Record total score for each skill)

Date	Visioning	Aligning

PROGRESS CHART

(Record total score for each skill)

Strategizing	Executing	Developing People

About Executive Foundation

What Is "Executive Foundation"?

Having worked with hundreds of clients and being former executives ourselves, we have found that successful executives have some indispensable traits in common. The successful executives we have observed all possess—or have acquired—a combination of skills, behaviors, and perspectives that drive great performance and results. It is these core skills, whether they come naturally or are learned, that we feel are the foundation of success, or what we call the "Executive Foundation."

The Five Key Skills for Executives to Master

The five essential skills we have identified—Visioning, Aligning, Strategizing, Executing, and Developing People—are higher-level executive functions. It is with these skills that executives grasp the big picture, create the culture of an organization, and drive their results.

It is also these five skills that determine a company's overall solvency. They are critical to

- successful positioning in the marketplace,
- efficiency, and
- productivity, and, as a result, to
- profitability, since it is the bottom line that benefits.

While there are many skills that are desirable for an executive to possess, we believe that a strong foundation in these five areas gives you the greatest probability of success. Many people make it to the executive ranks without mastering these key skills. Although it might seem counterintuitive, these skills are not the ones that are essential at the managerial level. Yet they are critical for the executive. We created this program both for the senior executive who wants to develop greater mastery as a leader and for the aspiring manager or junior executive who wants to develop the skills with which to succeed at the next level.

GETTING YOUR ARMS AROUND VISION

Although vision is actually a simple concept, it is one that many executives have trouble accepting the necessity of or understanding and putting into practice. What we have seen is that many executives make it more complex than it needs to be and therefore get stuck. Or, since it is an important but not urgent activity, which doesn't have the immediate pay-off other activities do, it is often neglected. The ultimate objective for the executive, however, is to envision, and then create, a viable long-term future for the business and organization that everyone can get excited about and rally around.

So, you might be thinking, how do I do that? We say keep it simple. Think of your vision for your business as the "desired future state" or "where you are going." Without a clear idea of your destination and route you may end up in the wrong place, or not get to where you need to go on time. It's really that simple. You don't need fancy statements or voluminous pages to describe a vision. The vision should be simple, meaningful, and memorable. By meaningful we mean not only important, but clearly linked to the purpose of your organization or company. By memorable we mean that you and others in the organization should be able to discuss your vision without referring to a written statement.

When a vision is meaningful you will find that you are excited about working to achieve it. So if you aren't excited about what you plan to undertake, then you need to re-evaluate and see what you can create that will spark some excitement. Remember, if it isn't exciting for you, then it will be difficult if not impossible to generate enthusiasm and excitement in others. And creating excitement is a key part of your job as you lead your organization.

It is also important that your vision reflect you and what you value. If it doesn't, this is another clue that you need to re-evaluate. If your values aren't represented fully in the vision, then you aren't bringing 100 percent of your leadership to it, which can be fatal for an organization or business trying to accomplish something big.

LINKING YOUR VISION TO YOUR VALUES

Values are deeply held views that we have acquired over a lifetime of experience. Although our values are at the core of who we are as individuals, they sometimes go unacknowledged.

Let's consider a leader who builds strong relationships with the people he works with closely. This simply comes naturally to him; he does not think of himself as valuing community, or deliberately cultivating it. If he were put in an environment or situation where building relationships was not the norm, however, he would most likely feel uncomfortable, and perhaps unsatisfied. That feeling of discomfort would be an indication that a key personal value was not being honored.

To help executives identify and articulate their values we have included a simple values inventory as part of Executive Foundation (See Appendix A). This inventory will help you identify your own four most important personal values. Now you can be sure to honor these values in your work.

Putting Your Vision on Paper

Many executives create elaborate vision statements that are too long and abstract to remember. If you can't state the vision simply, then it will be difficult for you to share it and for others to get excited about it. Most people need a call to action, which is what a vision provides. If it is simple, meaningful, and memorable, it can spearhead your organization in the direction you want it to take. Communicate your vision, verbally and in written form. Post it in visible places throughout your building and offices. Refer to it in speeches and presentations. This is what makes it real. This is how it becomes a shared vision.

Aligning to a Shared Vision

A shared vision is a vision that everyone buys into. You certainly can tell people what to do and expect them to follow. Telling people what to do is a traditional way of leading, which, especially in a crisis, when there's no time for debate, works. Yet, since you would not want to operate in crisis mode every day, or routinely avoid discussion, the ideal is to arrive at a shared vision. In fact, rather than working alone, you might decide to develop a vision with all of the managers who report directly to you, or with a subset of people from various parts of your organization. Once you have articulated your vision you will be ready to communicate it and can begin aligning your organization with the goals you have set out.

INCREASING ALIGNMENT

There are three essential keys to increasing alignment.

1. Build Relationships. The first thing an executive can do is to build relationships with key business partners and colleagues. This is critical to alignment. Most executives are good about aligning their direct staff but then make the mistake of thinking that everything else is in place and they are done. It's important to understand who in your company will be affected by what you are trying to accomplish. Many executives forget that they are not working in a silo but in a complex hierarchy in which their colleagues are focused on achieving their own goals. Meeting regularly is important and will allow you to hear firsthand their concerns and needs.

2. Link Business Processes to Vision. The second thing an executive can do to increase alignment is to link key business processes, such as business planning, performance management, compensation, and hiring, to the vision. Often a vision with well thought out strategies and goals can fail because the systems and processes needed to support it were simply not considered soon enough in the planning.

3. Create an Open Environment. The third action a leader can take to ensure alignment is to create an environment where people feel free to speak their minds. Ideally, you want people to bring up issues in a constructive and responsible way when things are going off track. This means you must establish trust not only among your direct report team, but also with your cross-functional teams, who may feel less comfortable speaking up, being critical, or offering advice.

So remember, it is building relationships throughout the organization, linking key business processes to the vision, and creating an atmosphere of openness and trust that lead to greater alignment.

HOW TO KNOW IF YOUR ORGANIZATION IS OUT OF ALIGNMENT

As soon as we talk about formulating a vision or striking out in a new direction we are talking about change. And talking about change is bound to provoke emotional reactions. So checking the emotional temperature of your organization is a great way to gauge how aligned people are. Emotions will run the gamut from fear to excitement. People may be cynical or angry about the anticipated changes, confused or simply overwhelmed. These feelings are natural and will run their course. But sometimes the negative emotions persist or escalate and can create resistance to what you are trying to accomplish. As a leader you need to watch out for this and take corrective action if necessary.

ACTIONS FOR BETTER ALIGNMENT

One of the best things you can do as a leader is to increase your visibility and improve communication within the organization. Get out of your office! Walk around. Talk informally to people at all levels. The second corrective action you can take is to turn up the volume of your communication, whether you accomplish this through general meetings, emails, or conference calls. Without open communication, negative emotions are more likely to dominate, and the more resistant or immobile people can become. You need to share details, explain the thinking behind your vision and goals, and demonstrate your enthusiasm for what you have laid out.

You want people to have a sense of moving forward, rather than to experience change as disruptive. In some cases, the organization has been through change before and it may not have been a positive experience Perhaps the executive didn't follow through with providing resources, communicating key information, or helping to build alignment for the change. So you need to think about what you can do to demonstrate your commitment to the vision and to include others in the change initiative.

OTHER SYMPTOMS OF BEING OUT OF ALIGNMENT

The following problems, all of which commonly occur in organizations, should be regarded as red flags that things are out of alignment:

- Confusion about roles and responsibilities. People don't know who is doing what. For things to run smoothly, it is important for everyone to know what their responsibilities are.

• Lack of enthusiasm and excitement. It makes sense that if people are unsure of what they're doing and don't know what is expected of them, they won't be excited about their work and the organization's goals. If they don't have a sense of how they fit into the bigger picture and are in the dark about what others are doing they may also be less than enthusiastic.

• Gossip. Gossip is a sign of unrest and uncertainty. People gossip when there is a void, when they are seeking information and there is not enough. What they don't know they often make up.

• Excessive or unproductive conflict. Another symptom that things are out of alignment is too much conflict. Creative tension is a good thing, but when increasing conflict gets in the way of results, you need to intervene. That may require you to re-emphasize the vision, clarify goals, and tighten up alignment with key partners. Often excessive conflict suggests that people are not clear about what's expected or do not have the resources (time, people or money) to get the job done. As we said earlier, the leader needs to be visible and to communicate regularly to keep people focused and enthusiastic.

WHY SPEND TIME ON STRATEGY?

Many executives are impatient to "just get into action and produce results." It is a common belief that planning and strategy development are only academic exercises that slow you down. However, we say you can't afford NOT to develop a strategy and plans. A strategy in business is the equivalent of the blueprint of a building. It's not impossible to build a building without a blueprint, but consider the disadvantages:

- It takes more time, since the steps are not laid out in advance.
- It's probably more expensive, since mistakes are likely to occur without a plan.
- It's unlikely to go smoothly, since how people's different roles will coordinate has not been anticipated and worked out.

So strategy is key. The bottom line is that a carefully considered strategy will save you time, money, and energy.

THE BUSINESS BLUEPRINT

The equivalent to a blueprint in business would be any of the following:

- Business plans
- Goals
- Contingency plans

Let's talk for a minute about a standard business plan. A good business plan should address some basic questions:

- What is our product/service?
- Who are our customers?
- Who are our other key
  business partners?
- How do we market to our
  customers?
- How do we price our services?
- How do we manage our expenses?
- What regulatory/legal issues do
  we need to manage?

As you analyze these questions and your business plan takes shape, you must also take into account three crucial considerations:

- Industry conditions
- Competition
- Possible obstacles

Considering these will help you not only clarify your goals and strategies but help you develop appropriate contingency plans.

So, once strategies and goals are in place, are you finished? No, strategy must always evolve and respond to current circumstances to be effective. Keeping that in mind, a strong leader encourages open discussion and debate about strategies. As you execute your plans and measure their success, you should be constantly reevaluating and fine-tuning both the strategy and the actions you've undertaken. If you are staying current with industry conditions, for example, then they should be reflected in your updated business plans and goals.

EXECUTING YOUR STRATEGIES AND PLANS

Many people have a good plan but fail to make it a reality. First and foremost, execution is about taking action — but not just any action. It must be action that is aligned with strategy. We all have seen situations where management teams seem to take a lot of action without producing results.

Secondly, successful execution requires monitoring the actions you take and assessing if they need to be changed. As we said earlier, a strategy is not a static thing. Monitoring action is critical so that your strategy can be fine-tuned according to how business unfolds.

And thirdly, successful execution depends on having the right resources at the right time. An executive who takes targeted action and is prepared to monitor it still needs the right resources for the task and must clearly specify who does what with the resources.

In summary, execution is not a "no brainer." It is not just a question of flooring the gas pedal. To execute a plan successfully you must

- Target the actions you take.
- Monitor actions. Don't assume things are proceeding as planned.
- Provide and match resources with actions that are clearly defined.

HOW POLICIES AND PROCEDURES AFFECT EXECUTION

Following the operating standards, norms, policies and procedures that you've established for your organization is key. Without them, the execution of strategies and plans often breaks down. Some organizations develop good policies and procedures but then don't actually use them. So, if you find that you have procedures that you aren't following, ask yourself if you have to go back and modify them. Are they what you really need? Are they too complicated? Or is it that you have not developed adequate policies and procedures to support your visions and plans?

MASTERING PEOPLE DEVELOPMENT

People development includes making the most of an individual's talent, bringing out someone's best, challenging people to deliver more than even they thought possible and then rewarding their success. When executives are not good at developing people the organization suffers. When people are not feeling fully utilized or valued for their contributions in an organization, they often leave. You get turnover, which is expensive. Or they try to get more attention by creating conflict, which means people are agitating, debating, and complaining rather than being productive. When executives fail to recognize and nurture creativity, that means they are missing opportunities to compete in the marketplace.

Some executives consider "people skills" the warm and fuzzy stuff and say that they're over rated. We say that bottom line what they accomplish is connection. When people feel connected to you as the leader, or connected to the company, they are more invested in its success. They work harder not because you tell them to but because they want to. So cultivating the people in an organization yields real and lasting results. We believe people development also means challenging people to go outside their comfort zone, to move to a higher level of performance. This means the leader must coach people, make big requests of people, and want more for them than they can see for themselves. At the same time, people need to know where they are going and be given some direction.

You might be thinking that in today's fast-paced business world people should be self-motivated and self-directed. Though, yes, it's great when people are self-motivated, there are two things to consider: (1) many people who are not self-motivated are still capable and productive with external direction; and (2) a leader's encouragement will make the performance of a self-motivated person even better. In the same way that superstar athletes appreciate athletic coaches, business people appreciate bosses who are good at coaching people – who listen, give feedback, motivate, inspire and build trust. In a company with that environment, people perform better, which goes right to bottom-line profitability.

MAKING TIME FOR EXECUTIVE FOUNDATION SKILLS

We recognize that working on the Executive Foundation skills may require time – time that you probably feel you don't have. Our book "Executive Think Time: Thinking That Gets Results" helps people do three things: (1) make the shift to valuing essential 'think time', (2) find ways to carve it out, even in a busy schedule, and, most important, (3) learn how best to use the time once they've got it. We provide a simple four–step model to help executives optimize their think time for better results. Executives who incorporate this approach will stop being reactive, find the time for things that they value, and have a base on which to build a stronger Executive Foundation.

MOVING FROM THE TACTICAL
TO THE STRATEGIC

In order to be strategic, you have to value the Executive Foundation skills and understand how they contribute to bottom-line results. Executives are tempted to cling to more tactical skills for various reasons:

- It's what got them promoted
- It's comfortable
- It's more concrete as a deliverable
- It's easier to show results

The five executive functions are more strategic in nature. They are important, but not urgent, as Covey says. If you skip them it doesn't show up today. But it will show up tomorrow. Executives often forget about tomorrow in the crisis of today.

HOW DO SUCCESSFUL EXECUTIVES THINK?

Most successful senior executives, by focusing time and energy on the five executive functions, have the advantages of

- a simple and memorable vision
- well-aligned teams
- a clear, well-articulated strategy
- a well thought-out plan that can be easily executed
- talented people with an investment in the company.

But they also have other strong qualities in common that contribute to their success. It's in the way they think. They take their work personally. They own their work and enjoy it. They are passionate about what they do and it matters to them that they make a serious contribution.

This is not the same as ego, or just wanting to be on top, although they do want that. It's a real set of values expressed in the attitude, "I'm a player, and I am here to play." Results matter. And it's not a spectator sport. They embody that quote from the basketball great Michael Jordan, who said, "I didn't come here to be average."

Another characteristic of successful executives is that they tend to be positive. They generally expect to be successful. They can't see any reason why they won't win because they have confidence, not just in their own talent, but in the talent of others. Because of this positive outlook, they tend to enjoy themselves. You can see that they like the game. They are engaged, fascinated. They're having fun.

We have also observed that many have a great ability to play to multiple audiences simultaneously. They are impressive from lots of angles, to their staff, to their bosses or board of directors, to their industry peers, and to the public. They have a 360° awareness and realize that all audiences are part of the game of business – staff, customers, peers, competitors, public.

Finally, they manage stress well because of the same traits that serve them well as leaders:

- They are not easily overwhelmed
- They keep their focus on the big picture. They do not attend to everything, just what matters most.
- They don't telegraph their concern. If they are worried or stressed, they express it in a way that mobilizes rather than alarms or discourages people.

BEYOND THE SKILLS OF
A SUCCESSFUL EXECUTIVE

There is one last thing that distinguishes successful executives.

What is it that the really outstanding leaders have

that other leaders do not? What is that quality attitude, or aura that successful leaders seem to radiate? It is something as an observer we often have difficulty describing, but we recognize it when we see it. We intuitively understand that this person is a powerful person, a leader. We call these elusive qualities "Executive Presence" and believe that successful executives possess presence in addition to their executive foundation and functional skills. Executive presence is acquired from the beliefs and attitudes with which an executive faces the world, as well as from experience. It can be felt in their physical presence and bearing as much as in their way of being. Stay tuned for our next book in which we will be exploring this in depth.

APPENDIX A
VALUES INVENTORY

Values as defined in the context of Executive Foundation are not moral values or principles. Values are the activities, preferences, or behaviors that you feel are important to you. They are things that you naturally gravitate towards and that come from within. Values are fundamentally who you are and what makes you tick. They are what sparks your passion, fills you with joy, and brings fulfillment. When you are clear about what you value and orient your life and work around them, you will feel more centered, grounded, and more at peace. When you are not honoring your values, you may feel internal tension, discomfort, or a dissonance.

Values should not be confused with a need. A need is something that you must have in order to be your best. Think of Maslow's hierarchy of needs: until the basics are met you can't be self actualized. It's the same with values. Until your needs are met, it's difficult to honor your values.

Why is it important for you as an executive, to be in touch with your values?

1. Values draw out natural charisma. When you are in touch with your values, you are being self-expressive. You bring 100% of your authentic self to work each day. When you show up as who you really are, others will find you more attractive and be naturally drawn to you and what you stand for. This makes your job as a leader much easier. You won't need to develop charisma because you will naturally have it.

2. Values give you clarity. When you know what you value, everything in life and business seems clearer. This clarity will provide order and support you to define a business vision, purpose, and goals.

3. Values keep you on track. As a leader you are faced with new opportunities and problems everyday. It's easy to go off track or to get overwhelmed with the choices that you face. When you honor your values, decision making is easier and your choices will stay aligned with your vision, purpose, and goals.

Being in touch with your values is natural motivation. They help keep you in action.

CLARIFYING YOUR VALUES

Many of you might be easily honoring your values everyday but not being aware of what they are. On the other side of the coin, you may be going through life on auto-pilot and not living congruently with your values.

Our objective is to help you identify what you value most. It's simple. Review the list of words below that represent values. This list is not all inclusive so feel free to add to the list. Circle the ten values that most appeal to you. If you get stuck, think about what others say about you or what you say about yourself.

An easy way to identify a value is to think about the times that you have felt an internal discord, discomfort, or an "out of integrity feeling".

ACCOMPLISHMENT	ACCURACY
ACKNOWLEDGEMENT	ADVENTURE
AESTHETICS	AUTHENTICITY
BEAUTY	CERTAINTY
COLLABORATION	COMMUNITY
CONNECTION	CONTRIBUTION
CONTROL	CREATIVITY

DUTY	EMPOWERMENT
EXCELLENCE	ELEGANCE
FAMILY	FREEDOM
FOCUS	FUN
GROWTH	HARMONY
HONESTY	HUMOR
INDEPENDENCE	INTEGRITY
INTIMACY	JOY
LEARNING	LOVE
LIGHTNESS	ORDER
PEACE	PERFORMANCE
PARTICIPATION	PLAY
PRODUCTIVITY	POWER
RECOGNITION	RISK TAKING
ROMANCE	SAFETY
SERVICE	SUCCESS
SPIRITUALITY	SELF EXPRESSION
TRADITION	TRUST

WORK

Once you have identified your values, rank them in order from 1 to 10 with 1 being the most important and 10 being the least important. Then ask yourself "do I honor these values everyday?" If not, look for ways to close the gap and incorporate the missing values into your day, both personally and professionally.

APPENDIX B – USING EXECUTIVE FOUNDATION FOR SUCCESSION PLANNING

Developing People is an essential skill for executives building their Executive Foundation. As a senior leader, succession planning is a key component of developing people for your organization's success. A well thought out succession plan ensures that you have a full and flowing pipeline of capable leaders ready to move up in the organization.

There are several transitions that an executive passes through on the way to the executive ranks. The book "The Leadership Pipeline" by Charan, Drotter and Noel, describe six passages:

Passage 1: Individual Contributor to Manager

Passage 2: Managing Others to Managing Managers

Passage 3: Managing Managers to Functional Manager

Passage 4: Functional Manager to Business Manager

Passage 5: Business Manager to Group Manager

Passage 6: Group Manager to Enterprise Manager

Each transition requires new skills to be successful at the new level. You need to determine what the specific skills are for your organization at each transition. The five essential skills found in Executive Foundation – Visioning, Strategizing/Planning, Aligning, Executing and Developing People - represent the core foundational skills used by leaders at all levels in the organization. Leaders that begin to develop and use these skills at the Manager level are more likely to have mastered these skills by the time they reach Phases 4 - 6. However, not all of the Executive Foundation skills are fully used and developed in Phases 2 - 3 in a leader's career progression.

As part of your succession planning, consider how the Executive Foundation skills can be developed and used at each career transition. It is important to think about the frequency and scope for each skill at each transition level. For example, the amount of time that a manager spends using each skill will be significantly less than the frequency of time that a Group Manager spends using that same skill. Likewise, the scope for use of the skill will be narrow at the Manager level and broaden as the leader moves up. Use the Executive Foundation assessment at each transition to determine the strength of your leaders. Aim for mastery by

Phase 3 – 4 so that your future executives have a firm foundation on which to run the business.

APPENDIX C
EXECUTIVE FOUNDATION FOR TEAMS:
CASE STUDY

The Executive Foundation Assessment is a great tool for individual leaders. We have also found that Executive Foundation is an excellent tool for teams of leaders who work together. Here is the story of a management team who successfully used Executive Foundation to develop the leadership skills of all six leaders on the team.

The Initial Goals

This is a manufacturing company which has an Operations Management team of six managers all reporting to the Vice President who is head of Operations. We started by individually coaching the Vice President of Operations. Through some feedback from his peers and internal customers, the Vice President learned that his team of six managers was well regarded and considered quite responsive to customers. However, what was also noticed by others was that his team did not seem to have much bench strength. There was no evident pipe line of future leaders. It was also not clear if the Operations unit had a clear vision or direction for the future. Since the company was growing, people felt it was important to have some sense that the Operations function was ready for and could handle the growth. Their specific strategy for the future was unclear.

So, based on this feedback from peers and internal customers, the Vice President of Operations led the initiative to have all six of his managers use Executive Foundation as a way to develop their skills. The three goals were 1) to improve people development skills, 2) improve vision skills, and 3) start thinking about a strategy for the future growth.

Team Coaching on Executive Foundation

We started our team coaching by having the team of six managers and the Vice President come together for our half-day Executive Foundation seminar. In that seminar we coached the group on how to develop the five key skills: visioning, aligning, strategizing, executing, and people development. The six managers also completed the Executive Foundation Assessment individually. We then coached each of the six managers to develop a personal development plan around the individual and specific skills they each wanted to strengthen.

Over the next three months the team was coached together. We met every other week and focused on each of the Executive Foundation skills one at a time. This made the skill development more focused and easier to embrace. Then, in between our team coaching sessions, the six managers practiced the Executive Foundation skills in their daily work with their own staff. At each team coaching session the managers shared both their successes and current challenges. So there was a great team building effect during the three month team coaching.

The Results

At the end of our three-month program, the six managers were asked to summarize how things had changed for them. These were some of the results they reported:

In addition to working on vision statements for their individual units, each manager had clarified their personal values around what leadership meant to them. So they had a clearer personal vision of their own role as a leader and how it fit into the total organization.

The managers admitted that they had been operating in silos and enjoyed coming together and finding that they had many challenges in common. In between team coaching meetings they started to ask each other's opinion more frequently. They consulted each other when problem solving. We felt this would lead to better integration of the operations functions down the road.

The managers really progressed on the skill of people development. They challenged their staff to a higher level of performance. They shared more information with their staff. They got clearer on their expectations of the staff. They empowered staff to make recommendations versus waiting for direction. The managers delegated more. Even the order of the staff meeting agendas were changed so that people issues were discussed before technical issues.

In terms of thinking about strategy, the team knew they needed to develop a clear, written strategic plan. The plan was still in progress and not completed during our three-month program. However, the team did report better planning of current work. The managers met with their peers outside of Operations more regularly and coordinated their actions better. This reduced some of the fire fighting. The managers were also starting to ask themselves better questions during planning. They questioned what the real priorities were, what work was really important, and how they could do things differently. So, we felt the foundation was in place to create a written strategy.

Overall, Executive Foundation proved to be an easy and valuable way to develop the entire team over a short period of time. The managers found it clear and practical. They also can return to the Executive Foundation assessment again and again to continue to develop their skills. In that way, their leadership development is ongoing.

Appendix D
Executive Foundation Distinctions

As a leader, language is a tool that we use everyday to think, communicate, inspire, and motivate. As coaches we are trained to help clients understand the subtleties of language, called distinctions, to create greater self awareness and enhance leadership. In this appendix are several distinctions to help build your executive foundation.

Vision versus Purpose: Vision is a picture or image of a desired future state. Purpose is why your organization exists or what it is here to do. Both are important to achieving results and motivating and aligning others.

Tactical versus Strategic: When you think tactically you are focused on the execution of plans and strategies. Your time horizon is the present. When thinking strategically, you are projecting into the future and determining what plans and actions will produce the results to be competitive and profitable. As an executive with a strong executive foundation, your goal is to strike a balance between tactical and strategic thinking. When your executive foundation is solid, you will spend more time on strategic thinking and less time on tactical matters.

Strategizing versus Planning: Think of strategizing as the "how" to get to where you want to be. Strategizing is often neglected because it is easier to jump right into action but a strong executive knows that strategizing is essential to sound execution. Planning is your roadmap to achieving your results. Executives who develop short and long term plans and goals are more proactive and appear to be in more control of their future.

Values versus Needs: Values should not be confused with a need. A need is something that you must have in order to be your best. Think of Maslow's hierarchy of needs: until the basics are met you can't be self actualized. It's the same with values. Until your needs are met, it's difficult to honor your values. Values are fundamentally who you are and what makes you tick. They are what sparks your passion, fills you with joy, and brings fulfillment. When you are clear about what you value, and orient your life and work around your values, you will feel more centered.

Agreement versus Alignment: As executives, you will be leading your organization in new directions and sometimes through change. It is not essential for others to agree with your vision, purpose, and plans. It is, however, essential that everyone be aligned with where you are headed. Leaders often mistake agreement for alignment. Alignment simply means that people will get behind your vision and plans and not do anything to undermine them. They don't have to like or agree with what you are doing but can still give 100%.

Doing versus Being: As a leader at the senior level, who you are being or your executive presence, is often more important than what you are doing. When you are at the top, people below you are always observing you. They immediately pick up on any lack of clarity or courage and see when you have gaps between "your walk and your talk". Make sure that you walk your talk.

ABOUT THE AUTHORS

Ellen Fredericks, Master Certified Coach, partners with executives, leaders, and business owners to take their individual, team or business performance to a new level. Her company, Partners in Possibility, specializes in supporting clients to build organizational cultures that reflect their vision and values and to develop leaders that can consistently produce new levels of results in the face of rapid change and competition. She also supports clients in the art of building powerful business relationships and cross-functional teams within a complex business structure.

Her clients include executives and leaders from start-up firms, not for profits and Fortune 500 companies including AT&T, IBM, Lucent Technologies, The United States Postal Service, Merck & Co., Pharmacia, Schering Plough, Prudential, UniLever, JP Morgan Chase, and others.

In addition to individual coaching, Ellen's professional services include group coaching, facilitation, and workshops on topics such as commitment leadership, emotional intelligence, relationship management, breakthrough thinking, and team effectiveness.

As a former corporate executive, Ellen brings twenty-five years of management and business experience to her coaching from the telecommunications industry where she held diverse positions in marketing, sales, information technology, operations, human resources, and government affairs. Her areas of business expertise include business management, business development, strategic planning, new product development, product marketing, and product management.

Ellen is one of several hundred coaches worldwide awarded the designation of Master Certified Coach by the International Coach Federation. Ellen holds an undergraduate degree in Computer Science and an advanced degree in Management. She attended Executive Management Training Programs at Duke University and Arizona State University.

In addition to her own coaching practice, Ellen is a coaching partner and the Vice President of Coaching for LBF InterCoach, Inc. She is the past President for the NJ Chapter of the International Coach Federation and the Founder and President of the New Jersey Institute of Technology (NJIT) Alumni Association Executive Program

Chapter. In 2001, she was featured as a leadership expert for the monster.com Leadership Center. Ellen is a contributing author to the recently published book, *Coaching for Extraordinary Results* (ASTD, 11/02).

CONTACT INFORMATION:

ellen@partnersinpossibility.com

About the Authors

Valerie Williams, Master Certified Coach, is an Executive Coach who runs her own company, "Professional Coaching and Training, Inc." Val presents training seminars to organizations and coaches executives individually to achieve career and personal goals. She specializes in Leadership, Strategic Planning, People Development, Team Development, and Stress Management. Val is a former corporate executive from the Managed Health Care Industry at Prudential Insurance. Val has managed staffs as large as 700 people. She was Executive Director of Prucare, the HMO of Northern New Jersey; Director of Prucare Customer Service Operations for the Northeast Region; and Director of Group Underwriting, Prucare of New York. Val has managed an annual operating budget of over 25 million dollars with direct impact on a network of 500,000 insured patients and 8,000 physicians and hospital providers.

Prior to her corporate career, Val worked with people on both physical and psychological rehab. Valerie earned a Bachelor of Science from Tufts University and a Master's Degree in Counseling Psychology from Boston University.

Leaders through the United States, France, Finland, England and Australia have worked with Val to raise the quality of their professional lives. Val coaches people (often by telephone) to develop greater focus and overcome obstacles so they can design the career and life they really want. In her seminars, Val is known for her interactive approach and practical style.

As a Coach, Val has presented seminars, facilitated management retreats and coached executives and professionals at a variety or corporations, universities, and professional organizations, including: Washington Mutual Bank, Bristol-Myers Squibb, TIAA-CREF, SBLI, General Electric, Prudential, National Utility Investors, American Express, Genentech, Pfizer, Harvard University, Pepsi, Nokia, University of Indianapolis, Horizon-Mercy HMO, AT&T, Lucent Technologies, Delta Dental, Schering-Plough, ADP, Women Unlimited and more.

As a leader in the coaching industry, Val is also a frequent speaker at coaching conferences nationwide.

Val was the first President for the New Jersey Chapter of the International Coach Federation. Val has been credentialed and awarded the designation "Master

Certified Coach" by the International Coaching Federation. Val has been featured in many publications, including *New York Newsday newspaper, Business Week, Economist, Executive Female Magazine, Black Enterprise, Essence magazine* and other healthcare magazines. Val has written two recently published books: *Get the Best Out of Your People and Yourself* and *Virtual Leadership.*

CONTACT INFORMATION:

val@valwilliams.com

Share It With Others

If you'd like to order more books, you can fill out this form and fax it to us at (877) 443-4092, or visit the website to email us and see other products: www.valwilliams.com

QTY	Product	Price	Total
	Executive Foundation	$12.95	
	Sales Tax: (NJ residents add 6%)		
	Shipping/Handling (Add $2.00 per book)		
	Total		

Shipping Address:

Name

Address 1

Address 2

City   State   Zip/Postal Code   Country

Phone   Fax

Email

Charge to:

Cardholder name

Credit Card Number   (Circle one):   Visa   Master Card   American Express

Expiration Date (MM/YY)

Fax completed order form to (877) 443-4092
If paying by check, mail check and completed form to:
Shadowbrook Publishing
PO Box 2458
Edison NJ 08818
Checks payable to Shadowbrook Publishing

TO ORDER
**Visit our websites: www.valwilliams.com or
www.partnersinpossibility.com**
or Fax 877.443.4092
(Our books are also available on Amazon.com)

- *Executive Think Time:*
  Thinking That Gets Results
  Most leaders are so busy, they don't take enough time
  to think. Ellen Fredericks and Val Williams wrote the
  book, *Executive Think Time: Thinking That Gets Results*
  This book gives leaders a simple, 4-step model to take
  their thinking to a higher level. A great solution for leaders
  who want to be less reactive and create results. 105 pages
  ($14.95 + $2 shipping)

- *Executive Think Time Training Seminars*
  Ellen Fredericks and Val Williams present on-site
  training seminars to roll out the 4-step Executive Think
  Time model to entire management teams. Seminars are
  customized to the organization's needs. Contact Ellen or
  Val for details.

- *Executive Foundation Coaching Programs*
  The assessment in this book shows executives both their
  strengths and areas for improvement in their executive skills.
  We also offer coaching programs designed for individuals
  and/or teams to strengthen leadership skills.

- *Other Books and Tapes by Val*
- ✓ *Get the Best Out of Your People and Yourself:*
  7 Practical Steps for Top Performance
  This book gives 7 practical steps for leaders and
  executives who want to see top performance from
  the staff. The handbook gives excellent practical
  instructions on delegation, giving feedback,
  performance management, and coaching your
  people. 100 pages ($14.95 + $2 shipping)

✓ *Virtual Leadership*
This little booklet gives leaders lots of tips for how to manage and coach their people when the staff is located in a different city or different country. When staff is in a different geographic location, how do you evaluate performance? coach performance? build a team? have successful teleconferences? This booklet gives solutions. 40 pages. ($6.95 + 1.50 shipping)

✓ *The Ways of Leadership* (Audiotape)
Strong Leadership is about more than what you "do." Real leadership is built on "who you are." ($10 + $1 shipping)

✓ *Building Your Personal Foundation*
7 Steps for a Happier Life (Audio CD)
Building your personal foundation will show you how to:
Raise your standards
Get your needs met
Eliminate what you tolerate
Restore integrity
Build boundaries
& more! ($10 + $1 shipping)

Shadowbrook Publishing
PO Box 2458, Edison NJ 08818
Fax 877.443.4092 • www.valwilliams.com